Happy 25th
Wedding Anniv

Love,
Bean & John

Much love,
Brett & Ann

The Wisdom of the Heart

The Wisdom of the Heart

A Celebration of Timeless Lessons
About Love

Compiled and Edited by Criswell Freeman

WALNUT GROVE PRESS
Nashville, TN 37205

ISBN 1-887655-34-4

The ideas expressed in this book are not, in all cases, exact quotations, as some have been edited for clarity and brevity. In all cases, the author has attempted to maintain the speaker's original intent. In some cases, material for this book was obtained from secondary sources, primarily print media. While every effort was made to ensure the accuracy of these sources, the accuracy cannot be guaranteed. For additions, deletions, corrections or clarifications in future editions of this text, please write WALNUT GROVE PRESS.

Printed in the United States of America
Cover Design by Mary Mazer
Typesetting & Page Layout by Sue Gerdes
Editor for Walnut Grove Press: Alan Ross
4 5 6 7 8 9 10 •   00 01

ACKNOWLEDGMENTS
The author gratefully acknowledges the helpful support of Laura Balthrop, Angela Beasley, Dick and Mary Freeman, and Mary Susan Freeman.

For Angela

Table of Contents

Introduction

Since the beginning of history, man has attempted to define love with decidedly mixed results. Perhaps this difficulty is to be expected since the word "love" does not denote a single phenomenon. The English language contains several hundred words and phrases which describe various aspects of devotion, affection attraction, and infatuation. No one definition suffices.

Love can be directed inward, outward or (hopefully) in both directions. Love is friendship, but it is also passion. The word applies to puppy love as well as to the love of puppies. For some, love means family, for others it means worship. To some, love is exclusively physical, to others, purely spiritual. It is small wonder that love, perhaps the most paradoxical of human experiences, sometimes confounds even the most seasoned experts.

This book does not answer every question concerning the mysteries of amour. An encyclopedia would be insufficient for that task. Instead, the pages that follow comprise a brief catalogue of thought-provoking quotations. As you read these words, apply them to your own life and embark upon the ultimate adventure: the exploration of the human heart.

1

Love Is...

While considering matters of the heart, Franklin P. Jones observed, "Love doesn't make the world go 'round, but love is what makes the ride worth while." Amen to those sentiments. But what form of love was Jones describing? There's no telling. Love means different things at different times to different people. In this chapter we explore the manifold meanings of history's most important four-letter word. Enjoy the ride.

Life is the flower of which love is the honey.

Victor Hugo

A man is not where he lives,
but where he loves.

Latin Proverb

Life's greatest happiness is to be convinced
we are loved.

Victor Hugo

Love is the subtlest force in the world.

Mohandas Gandhi

Love is life .... And if you miss love,
you miss life.

Leo Buscaglia

Love Is...

Tell me whom you love, and I will tell you
what you are.

Arsène Houssaye

Love is the strongest force
the world possesses, and yet
it is the humblest imaginable.

Mohandas Gandhi

It is love that asks, that seeks, that knocks,
that finds, and that is faithful
to what it finds.

St. Augustine

To love at all is to be vulnerable.

C. S. Lewis

Love is a great beautifier.

Louisa May Alcott

Love is trembling happiness.

Kahlil Gibran

Love is the everlasting possession
of the good.

Plato

Love is the irresistible desire
to be desired irresistibly.

Louis Ginzberg

Love is a game
that two can play
and both win.

Eva Gabor

A pennyweight o' love is worth
a pound o' law.

Scottish Proverb

We define love as a delight in the presence
of the other person and an affirming
of his value and development
as much as one's own.

Rollo May

We are all born for love; it is the principle
of existence and its only end.

Benjamin Disraeli

Falling in love is the one illogical adventure,
the one thing which we are tempted to think
of as supernatural, in our trite
and reasonable world.

Robert Louis Stevenson

Love is space and time made directly
perceptible to the heart.

Proust

Love is ever the beginning of knowledge
as fire is of light.

Thomas Carlyle

Love, like death, changes everything.

Kahlil Gibran

Love is union under the condition
of preserving one's integrity.

Erich Fromm

And now abideth faith, hope, love,
these three; but the greatest of these
is love.

I Corinthians 13:13

Love is the essence of God.

Ralph Waldo Emerson

Where love is, there is God also.

Leo Tolstoy

Love is patient and kind; love is not jealous, or conceited, or proud; love is not ill-mannered, or selfish, or irritable; love does not keep a record of wrongs; love is not happy with evil, but is happy with the truth. Love never gives up: its faith, hope and patience never fail.

I Corinthians 13:4-7

Love is my decision to make your problem
my problem.

Robert Schuller

Love is spontaneous and craves expression
through joy, through beauty, through truth,
even through tears. Love lives the moment;
it's neither lost in yesterday nor does
it crave for tomorrow.
Love is now.

Leo Buscaglia

Love is the ultimate and the highest goal
to which man can aspire.

Viktor Frankl

Love doesn't drop on you unexpectedly;
you have to give off signals, sort of like
an amateur radio operator.

Helen Gurley Brown

Love is but the discovery of ourselves
in others, and the delight in the recognition.

Alexander Smith

Love is the crowning grace of humanity,
the holiest right of the soul.

Petrarch

Love is living the experience of another
person in all his uniqueness and singularity.

Viktor Frankl

Love is the only sane and satisfactory answer to the problems of human existence.

Erich Fromm

I define love thus: the will to extend
one's self for the purpose of nurturing
one's own or another's spiritual growth.

M. Scott Peck

Love is an impulse which springs from the
most profound depths of our beings, and
upon reaching the visible surface of life
carries with it an alluvium of shells and
seaweed from the inner abyss.

José Ortega y Gasset

Love is a multiplication.

Marjory Stoneman Douglas

Love is not enough, but is sure helps.

Sheldon Kopp

2

Self-Love

Leo Buscaglia notes, "Who is the loving person? The loving person is the one who loves himself or herself." If there is a single overriding prerequisite for loving another human being, that prerequisite is self-love.

Healthy self-love is not narcissism nor is it conceit. Instead, it is a strong sense of one's innate worthiness. Without healthy self-love, the ability to care for others is inevitably frustrated.

If you wish to gain more from your relationships, begin by celebrating the person in the mirror. And then turn the page.

Love yourself first.

Lucille Ball

If you can't stand yourself, neither can anybody else.

Sid Caesar

One cannot give what he does not possess.
To give love you must possess love.
To love others you must love yourself.

Leo Buscaglia

He who is able to love himself is able
to love others also.

Paul Tillich

Nothing can bring you peace but yourself.

Ralph Waldo Emerson

There is a rare beauty that comes from the soul.
Beauty comes from within.

Eva Gabor

Happiness cannot come from without. It must come from within.

Helen Keller

Good temper,
like a sunny day,
sheds light
on everything.

Washington Irving

The deepest need of man, then, is the need
to overcome his separateness, to leave
the prison of his aloneness.

Erich Fromm

All life itself represents a risk,
and the more lovingly we live our lives,
the more risks we take.

M. Scott Peck

In my relationships with others, I have found
that it does not help, in the long run,
to act as though I were something
I am not.

Carl Rogers

Love is, above all, the gift of oneself.

Jean Anouilh

To live happily is an inward joy of the soul.
Marcus Aurelius

It is true that selfish persons are incapable
of loving others, but they are not capable
of loving themselves either.
Erich Fromm

So much of what you are *not* is because
you are literally standing in your own way
of becoming.
Leo Buscaglia

Perhaps love is the process of my leading you gently back to yourself.

Antoine de Saint-Exupéry

We are never more discontented
with others than when we are discontented
with ourselves.

Henri Frédéric Amiel

Selfishness and self-love, far from being
identical, are actually opposites.

Erich Fromm

Peace of mind really comes out of the
harmony of life. Peace of mind is another way
of saying that you've learned how to love,
that you have come to appreciate the
importance of giving love in order
to be worthy of receiving it.

Hubert H. Humphrey

An inexhaustible good nature is one
of the most precious gifts of heaven.

Washington Irving

The hardest battle you're ever going to fight
is the battle to be just you.

Leo Buscaglia

To thine own self be true.

William Shakespeare

The affirmation of one's own life, happiness, growth, freedom, is rooted in one's capacity to love.

Erich Fromm

Though we travel
the world over to find
the beautiful, we must
carry it with us,
or we find it not.

Ralph Waldo Emerson

3

Love in Action

It is commonly assumed that love is a feeling, but this assumption is misguided. Infatuation is a feeling. Genuine love is a behavior. Shakespeare wrote, "They do not love that do not show it." This fact forms the bedrock of all loving relationships.

To profess love is easy, but to act in a loving fashion is sometimes very hard. When we're tired, angry, frustrated, frightened or jealous, the will to hurt may outweigh the will to help. But a wise person resists the easy temptation of cruelty. Instead, he or she behaves lovingly even when the feeling of love seems only a distant memory.

If you're seeking a sure-fire way to improve your relationships, try a time-tested technique: Let the actions of love speak even more loudly than the words. Despite notions to the contrary, the real proof of love is in the doing, not the wooing.

Love is shown by deeds, not by words.

Philippine Proverb

Love is not only something you feel.
It's something you do.

David Wilkerson

Love is as strict as acting. If you want to love
somebody, stand there and do it. If you don't,
don't. There are no other choices.

Tyne Daly

If one wishes to know love, one must live love,
in action.

Leo Buscaglia

Love is an act of will — namely, both an
intention and an action. Will also implies
choice. We do not have to love.
We choose to love.

M. Scott Peck

Love is an activity, not a passive affect; it is a "standing in," not a "falling for."

Erich Fromm

It is no profit to have learned well, if you neglect to do well.

Publilius Syrus

Love, in its very essence, is choice.

José Ortega y Gasset

Love is responsibility.

Martin Buber

Love also presupposes freedom.
Certainly love which is not freely given
is not love.

Rollo May

The way to love anything is to realize
that it might be lost.

G. K. Chesterton

Whoever loves true life, will love true love.
Elizabeth Barrett Browning

Loving is something more serious and
significant than being excited by the lines
of a face and the color of a cheek.
It is a decision.

José Ortega y Gasset

Love does not begin and end the way
we seem to think it does. Love is a battle,
love is a war; love is growing up.

James Baldwin

Great loves too must be endured.

Coco Chanel

Love is a force. It is not a result;
it is a cause. It is not a product. It is a power,
like money, or steam or electricity.
It is valueless unless you can give
something else by means of it.

Anne Morrow Lindbergh

There is no love where there is no will.

Mohandas Gandhi

Nothing is impossible to a willing heart.

John Heywood

Love many things, for therein lies the true
strength, and whosoever loves much
performs much, and can accomplish much,
and what is done in love is well done.

Vincent van Gogh

Habit is everything — even in love.

Vauvenargues

The giving of love is an education in itself.

Eleanor Roosevelt

We can only learn to love by loving.

Iris Murdoch

Love must be learned again and again;
there is no end to it. Hate needs
no instruction.

Katherine Anne Porter

Genuine love is volitional
rather than emotional.

M. Scott Peck

4

Love Grows

Love, like a young seedling, grows best under certain conditions. In this chapter, wise men and women advise us on the proper care and feeding of relationships. So go and sow ... and grow.

Love is primarily giving, not receiving.

Erich Fromm

Love, and you shall be loved. All love is mathematical, just as much as the two sides of an algebraic equation.

Ralph Waldo Emerson

Love isn't like a reservoir. You'll never drain it dry. It's much more like a natural spring. The longer and the farther it flows, the stronger and the deeper and the clearer it becomes.

Eddie Cantor

There is no greater invitation to love than loving first.

St. Augustine

To be loved, love.

Decimus Maximus Ausonius

If you'd be loved, be worthy to be loved.

Ovid

To get the full value of joy, you have to have someone to divide it with.

Mark Twain

We are shaped and fashioned
by what we love.

Goethe

Since love is not a thing, it is not lost when given. You can offer your love completely to hundreds of people and still retain the same love you had originally.

Leo Buscaglia

We receive love not in proportion to our demands or sacrifices or needs, but roughly in proportion to our own capacity to love.

Rollo May

The one thing we can never get enough of
is love. And the one thing we never give
enough of is love.

Henry Miller

Immature love says: "I love you because
I need you." Mature love says: "I need you
because I love you."

Erich Fromm

Each partner should take full responsibility
for improving the relationship.

Aaron Beck

One does not fall "in" or "out" of love.
One grows in love.

Leo Buscaglia

Love dies only when growth stops.

Pearl Buck

Inasmuch as love grows in you,
so beauty grows. For love is the beauty
of the soul.

St. Augustine

Familiarity, truly cultivated, can breed love.

Dr. Joyce Brothers

Love does not dominate;
it cultivates.

Goethe

Love goes to those who are deserving —
not to those who set snares for it and who
lie in wait. The life of strife and contest
never wins.

Elbert Hubbard

Love gives itself; it is not bought.

Henry Wadsworth Longfellow

The joy of life is variety;
the tenderest love requires to be renewed
by intervals of absence.

Samuel Johnson

Remember the old saying:
    "Faint heart ne'er won fair lady."

Miguel de Cervantes

To live in love is life's greatest challenge.
It requires more subtlety, flexibility, sensitivity,
understanding, acceptance, tolerance,
knowledge, and strength than any other human
endeavor or emotion.

Leo Buscaglia

There is no remedy for love
    but to love more.

Henry David Thoreau

Alas, oh, love is dead!
How could it perish thus? No one has cared for
it: It simply died of frost.

Angelus Silesius

Love it the way it is.

Thaddeus Golas

5

Romance and Passion

In 1665, La Rochefoucauld wrote, "The passions are the only orators which always persuade." But he might have added that passion, while a powerful persuader, is not always a wise one.

American actress Bette Davis observed, "Love is not enough. It must be the foundation, the cornerstone, but not the complete structure. It is much too pliable, too yielding."

Both Davis and La Rochefoucauld were correct. Passion lights the fire, but compassionate people must tend it.

For those passionately in love,
the whole world seems to smile.

David Myers

Without passion man is mere latent force,
like the flint which awaits the shock of the
iron before it can give forth its spark.

Henri Frédéric Amiel

Love is the fire of life; it either consumes
or purifies.

Anonymous

The heart has its reasons which reason
does not know.

Pascal

The heart is forever inexperienced.

Henry David Thoreau

Let my heart be wise.
It is the gods' best gift.

Euripides

The best and most beautiful things in the world cannot be seen or even touched. They must be felt with the heart.

Helen Keller

Seeing's believing, but feeling's the truth.

Thomas Fuller

When we are in love, we often doubt
what we most believe.

La Rochefoucauld

Where the heart lies, let the brain lie also.

Robert Browning

Passion, though a bad regulator,
is a powerful spring.

Ralph Waldo Emerson

If the world is cold, make it your business
to build fires.

Horace Traubel

When people are infatuated, they tend
to read into the partner all kinds of positive
qualities that are not present, or are present
in a lesser degree than they imagine.

Aaron Beck

Too much love causes heartbreak.

Philippine Proverb

Passion goes, boredom remains.

Coco Chanel

Serving one's own passions
is the greatest slavery.

Thomas Fuller

Passion is a bad counselor.

Thomas Hardy

Do not believe hastily. What harm quick belief can do.

Ovid

Hot love is soon cold.

English Proverb

Guard thy sail from passion's sudden blast.

Charles Simmons

No one has ever loved anyone the way
everyone wants to be loved.

Mignon McLaughlin

In real love you want the other person's good.
In romantic love you want the other person.

Margaret Anderson

Never idealize others. They will never live
up to your expectations. Don't over-analyze
your relationships. Stop playing games.
A growing relationship can only
be nurtured by genuineness.

Leo Buscaglia

Infatuation has been likened to an addiction.

Aaron Beck

Either you master your emotions
or they master you. Uncontrolled love
can burn you out.

Loretta Young

True love is not a feeling by which we are
overwhelmed. It is a committed,
thoughtful decision.

M. Scott Peck

Love is an ideal thing, marriage a real thing;
a confusion of the real with the ideal
never goes unpunished.

Goethe

The rational mind cultivates all human interests in undue proportion. The lovesick dreamland dear to irrational poets is a distorted image of the ideal world.

George Santayana

Love has a tide.

Helen Hunt Jackson

Love and hatred are natural exaggerators.

Hebrew Proverb

You have to work constantly at rejuvenating a relationship. You can't just count on its being OK, or it will tend toward a hollow commitment, devoid of passion and intimacy.

Dr. Robert Sternberg

Life is a romantic business, but you have to make the romance.

Oliver Wendell Holmes, Sr.

In nine cases out of ten, a woman had better
show more affection than she feels.

Jane Austen

Women are never what they seem to be.
There is the woman you see, and there is
the woman who is hidden. Buy the gift
for the woman who is hidden.

Erma Bombeck

It is better to be looked over
than to be overlooked.

Mae West

6

Kindness

Mark Twain noted, "Kindness is the language which the deaf can hear and the blind can see." Before his death, Twain was able to see his words put into action by the indefatigable Helen Keller. Despite losing both sight and hearing at the age of 19 months, Keller personified the spirit of loving-kindness. She once observed, "Life is an exciting business and most exciting when lived for others." Helen loved the world, and the world loved back. It always does.

Both Twain and Keller understood that an immutable law applies to all humanity: If we wish to be loved, we must be kind; and if we are kind, we will be loved.

Kindness is the language of genuine love. Thankfully, it's a language that needs no translation.

Kindness

The way to make yourself pleasing to others
is to show that you care for them. The seeds
of love can never grow but under the warm
and genial influence of kind feelings
and affectionate manners.

William Wirt

He who sows courtesy reaps friendship,
and he who plants kindness reaps love.

Richard Brooks

Scatter seeds of kindness.

George Ade

Kindness in giving creates love.

Lao-tzu

Life is short and we never
have enough time for
the hearts of those who
travel the way with us.
O, be swift to love!
Make haste to be kind.

Henri Frédéric Amiel

None is so near the gods as he
who shows kindness.

Seneca

To love is to give one's time.
We never give the impression that we care
when we are in a hurry.

Paul Tournier

The only gift is a portion of thyself.

Ralph Waldo Emerson

We must not only give what we *have*;
we must also give what we *are*.

Désiré-Joseph Cardinal Mercier

All who would win joy
must share it; happiness
was born a twin.

Lord Byron

Love is not just some great abstract idea
or feeling. There are some people with such
a lofty conception of love that they never
succeed in expressing it in the simple
kindnesses of ordinary life.

Paul Tournier

When you're not thinking about yourself,
you're usually happy.

Al Pacino

Love is not getting, but giving.

Henry Van Dyke

Love seeks one thing only: the good of the
one loved. It leaves all the other secondary
effects to take care of themselves.
Love, therefore, is its own reward.

Thomas Merton

Familiar acts are beautiful through love.

Percy Bysshe Shelley

The best portion of a good man's life:
his little, nameless, unremembered acts
of kindness and of love.

William Wordsworth

Be completely humble and gentle;
be patient bearing with one another in love.

Ephesians 4:2

If you have a voice, sing; if your limbs
are supple, dance. In fact, do not neglect
any means of giving pleasure.

Ovid

It's a bit embarrassing to have been
concerned with the human problem all one's
life and find at the end that one has no more
to offer by way of advice than
"Try to be a little kinder."

Aldous Huxley

The best cure for worry, depression,
melancholy, brooding, is to go deliberately
forth and try to lift with one's sympathy
the gloom of somebody else.

Arnold Bennett

If something comes to life in others because
of you, then you have made an approach
to immortality.

Norman Cousins

If you mean to profit, learn to please.

Charles Churchill

Charm is simply this: the golden rule,
good manners, good grooming, good humor,
good sense, good habits, and a good outlook.

Loretta Young

If you want to gather honey,
don't kick over the beehive.

Dale Carnegie

He who receives a benefit should never
forget it; he who bestows should
never remember it.

Pierre Charron

Never lose a chance of saying a kind word.

William Makepeace Thackeray

No act of kindness, no matter how small,
is ever wasted.

Aesop

You can give without loving, but you
cannot love without giving.

Amy Carmichael

There is no love which does not become help.

Paul Tillich

Kind words can be short and easy to speak, but their echoes are truly endless.

Mother Teresa

7

Communication

Some of us are good talkers but poor listeners; for others, the reverse is true. But the growth of a loving relationship requires that we do both.

To become a good communicator, one must first become a good listener. M. Scott Peck notes, "The principal form that the work of love takes is attention. When we love another we give him or her our attention; we attend to the person's growth." Peck added, "True listening is love in action." But there is more to love than simply listening; we must also share our own feelings. This too is difficult.

On the following pages, we consider the gentle art of effective, two-way communication. It is the most delicate work of love.

The first duty of love is to listen.

Paul Tillich

There is only one rule for being
a good talker — learn how to listen.

Christopher Morley

Know how to listen, and you will profit
even from those who talk badly.

Plutarch

When a woman is speaking to you,
listen to what she says with her eyes.

Victor Hugo

Be a good listener. Your ears will never get
you in trouble.

Frank Tyger

You can't fake listening.

Raquel Welch

The sweetest of all sounds is praise.

Xenophon

When someone does something good, applaud! You'll make two people happy.

Sam Goldwyn

If they want peace, nations should avoid
the pinpricks that precede cannon shots.

Napoleon

Keep the other person's well-being in mind
when you feel an attack of soul-purging truth
coming on.

Betty White

When you shoot an arrow of truth,
dip its point in honey.

Arab Proverb

Never, never, never be a cynic,
even a gentle one.

Vachel Lindsay

It is not the desert island nor the stony
wilderness that cuts you off from the people
you love. It is the wilderness in the mind,
the desert wastes in the heart through
which one wanders lost and a stranger.

Anne Morrow Lindbergh

Please don't wait to communicate your
feelings. One of the greatest destructive
elements in relationships and intimacy is our
inability to relate what we're feeling now.

Leo Buscaglia

We can only love what we know,
and we can never know completely
what we do not love.

Aldous Huxley

Never close your lips to those to whom
you have opened your heart.

Charles Dickens

Every person's feelings have a front door
and a side door by which
they may be entered.

Oliver Wendell Holmes, Sr.

Beware of the danger signals that flag
problems: silence, secretiveness,
or sudden outburst.

Sylvia Porter

Misunderstanding is often an active
process that results when one partner
develops a distorted picture of the other.

Aaron Beck

Happiness, grief, gaiety, sadness,
are by nature contagious.

Henri Frédéric Amiel

8

Forgiveness

Two thousand years ago, Ovid wrote, "Lovers remember all things." Very little has changed since then. Lovers have sharp memories, sometimes too sharp.

When we focus on yesterday's troubles, we do continuing harm to our loved ones and ourselves. For this reason, it is important to learn the art of forgiveness.

Forgiveness is not a one-time event. As human beings, we can't simply "forgive and forget"; we're not wired that way. But we *can* decide to initiate the *process* of forgiving. This process begins when we make the conscious decision to fight hatred every time it invades the heart. Eventually, after many episodes of backsliding, love wins out. The great irony of forgiveness is that it is circular: When we forgive others, we liberate ourselves.

If you're imprisoned by anger or resentment, begin planning your escape. Freedom is always beautiful. And so is forgiveness.

Hatred darkens life; love illuminates it.
Martin Luther King, Jr.

Bitterness imprisons life; love releases it.
Harry Emerson Fosdick

Forgiveness is the final form of love.
Reinhold Niebuhr

Look upon the errors of others in sorrow,
not in anger.
Henry Wadsworth Longfellow

Life is an exercise in forgiveness.

Norman Cousins

The loving person has no need to be perfect,
only human.

Leo Buscaglia

Perfect love means to love the one through
whom one became unhappy.

Kierkegaard

I have decided to stick with love.
Hate is too great a burden to bear.

Martin Luther King, Jr.

Suffering is the true cement of love.

Paul Sabatier

Love truth and pardon error.

Voltaire

Force may subdue, but love gains, and he
who forgives first wins the laurel.

William Penn

A retentive memory is a good thing,
but the ability to forget is the true token
of greatness.

Elbert Hubbard

Love covereth a multitude of sins.

I Peter 4:8

Hate the sin and love the sinner.

Mohandas Gandhi

We can forgive as long as we love.

La Rochefoucauld

Love is an act of endless forgiveness,
a tender look which becomes a habit.

Peter Ustinov

Forget injuries,
never forget
kindnesses.

Confucius

The art of being wise is knowing what to overlook.

William James

9

Friendship

Loving relationships are best built upon the firm foundation of friendship. On the pages that follow, we consider what it means to be a friend. Emerson wrote, "A friend may well be reckoned the masterpiece of nature."

And a friend may well be reckoned the *centerpiece* of love.

A faithful friend is the medicine of life.

Old Proverb

Friendship is a single soul living in two bodies.

Aristotle

Other people are like a mirror which
reflects back on us the kind of image we cast.

Bishop Fulton J. Sheen

When you love your neighbor,
then you are like unto God.

Kierkegaard

The only way to have a friend is to be one.

Ralph Waldo Emerson

A friend should bear his friend's infirmities.
William Shakespeare

Shared joys make a friend,
not shared sufferings.
Nietzsche

Friendship flourishes at the fountain
of forgiveness.
William Arthur Ward

There is no wilderness like a life
without friends.

Baltasar Gracián

The worst solitude is to be destitute
of sincere friendship.

Francis Bacon

The deepest principle of human nature
is the craving to be appreciated.

William James

True friendship is self-love at secondhand.

William Hazlitt

Life is partly what we make it and partly what is made by the friends we choose.

Chinese Proverb

Among those whom I like or admire,
I can find no common denominator,
but among those whom I love, I can:
All of them make me laugh.

W. H. Auden

So long as we love, we serve. So long as we
are loved by others, I would almost say we
are indispensable; and no man is useless
while he has a friend.

Robert Louis Stevenson

The time to be happy is now.
The way to be happy is to make others so.

Robert Ingersoll

All the law is fulfilled in one word,
even in this: Thou shalt love thy neighbor
as thyself.

Galatians 5:14

10

Jealousy

An old English proverb states that "the course of true love never did run smooth." And when the course of true love becomes bumpy, jealousy usually provides the bumps.

Jealousy comes in many shapes and sizes. We may be jealous of another person, or we may be jealous of our loved one's work. We can be jealous of hobbies, friends, family members, even over-used television sets.

Whatever its cause, jealousy is always destructive because it tends to be self-fulfilling. The more jealous we become, the more we drive away the person whose affections we seek. Jealousy masquerades as love, but in truth, it more closely resembles fear than caring.

If your relationships are a little bumpy, consider the ideas that follow. As you smooth out your jealous feelings, you'll pave the way to genuine love.

Jealousy is the great exaggerator.

Schiller

It is not love that produces jealousy —
it is selfishness.

Justice Wallington

In jealousy there is more of self-love
than love.

La Rochefoucauld

Jealousy is a mental cancer.

B. C. Forbes

Love that is fed by jealousy dies hard.

Ovid

Jealousy is always born with love,
but does not always die with it.

La Rochefoucauld

Love is the child of freedom,
    never that of domination.

Erich Fromm

One cannot be a lover by force.

Turkish Proverb

Love is like quicksilver in the hand. Leave
the fingers open and it stays in the palm;
clutch it, and it darts away.

Dorothy Parker

Love is trusting.

Leo Buscaglia

The person who pursues revenge should dig
two graves.

Old Proverb

When anger rises, think of the consequences.

Confucius

Never do anything when you are in a temper,
for you will do everything wrong.

Baltasar Gracián

Anger is a wind which blows out the lamp
of the mind.

Robert Ingersoll

Can there be a love which does not make
demands on its object?

Confucius

The jealous person engenders the very thing
he fears: the withdrawal of love.

Viktor Frankl

It takes patience to appreciate domestic bliss;
volatile spirits prefer unhappiness.

George Santayana

Love is generally confused with dependence;
but in point of fact, you can love only in
proportion to your capacity for independence.

Rollo May

Love is always open arms. With arms open
you allow love to come and go as it will, freely,
for it'll do so anyway. If you close your arms
about love, you'll find you are left
only holding yourself.

Leo Buscaglia

Sing and dance together and be joyous,
but let each one also be alone.

Kahlil Gibran

Him that I love, I wish to be free —
even from me.

Anne Morrow Lindbergh

P artners need, first of all, to realize that
much of the friction between them is due
to misunderstandings stemming from
differences in their perspectives — and is
not the result of meanness or selfishness.

Aaron Beck

I f you judge people, you have no time
to love them.

Mother Teresa

S earch thine own heart. What paineth thee
in others in thyself may be.

John Greenleaf Whittier

O nly the person who has faith in himself
is able to be faithful to others.

Erich Fromm

Jealousy

Give me such love for God and men as
   will blot out all hatred and bitterness.
                              Dietrich Bonhoeffer

See everything; overlook a great deal;
            correct a little.
                              Pope John XXIII

Growth in wisdom may be exactly measured
         by decrease in bitterness.
                              Nietzsche

You can't have a better tomorrow if you
      are always thinking about yesterday.
                              Charles F. Kettering

Hating people is like burning down
      your own house to get rid of a rat.
                              Harry Emerson Fosdick

The jealous are
troublesome to others,
but a torment
to themselves.

William Penn

Sadness is almost never
anything but a form
of fatigue.

André Gide

11

Cooperation

Love flourishes in an atmosphere of constant cooperation. Conversely, wherever there is selfishness, love is not.

Antoine de Saint-Exupéry wrote, "Life has taught us that love does not consist in gazing at each other but in looking outward together in the same direction." In this chapter, we consider lessons in cooperation. Why are these lessons important? Because two people pulling in opposite directions go nowhere.

Nothing great was ever achieved
without enthusiasm.

Ralph Waldo Emerson

Bring your health and your strength to the
weak and sickly, and so you will be of use to
them. Give them, not your weakness, but your
energy, so you will revive and lift them up.
Life alone can rekindle life.

Henri Frédéric Amiel

We live very close together.
So, our prime purpose in this life is to help
others. And if you can't help them
at least don't hurt them.

The Dalai Lama

Hope is the mainspring of life.

Henry Stimson

Never take away hope from any human being.

Oliver Wendell Holmes, Sr.

To love means to decide independently
to live with an equal partner, and to
subordinate oneself to the formation
of a new subject, a "we."

Fritz Kunkel

Love cannot be commanded.

Latin Proverb

No one loves the man whom he fears.

Aristotle

Where love rules, there is no will to power;
and where power predominates, there love
is lacking. The one is the shadow of the other.

Carl Jung

Your spouse is your closest relative and is entitled to depend on you as a common ally, supporter, and champion.

Aaron Beck

Love is not an emotion — love is a relationship.

Rudolf Dreikurs

Discover someone to help shoulder your misfortunes. Then, you will never be alone. Neither fate, nor the crowd, so readily attacks two.

Baltasar Gracián

Never cease to be convinced that life might be better — your own and others'.

André Gide

Love gives itself, but is not bought.
Henry Wadsworth Longfellow

Duty does not have to be dull.
Love can make it beautiful and fill it with life.
Thomas Merton

As passions subside after the initial
infatuation, dedication to each other's welfare
and happiness emerge as the major binding
forces in a relationship.
Aaron Beck

A lady of 47, who has been married 27 years
and has six children, knows what love really is
and once described it for me like this: "Love is
what you've been through with somebody."
James Thurber

I love my work, but work itself
      doesn't add up to happiness.
      Happiness is sharing a life.

Michael Landon

Talk happiness. The world is sad enough
      without your woes.

Ella Wheeler Wilcox

The fault-finder will find faults
      even in paradise.

Henry David Thoreau

Misery is a communicable disease.

Martha Graham

Love becomes help.

Paul Tillich

Nothing we do, however virtuous, can be accomplished alone; therefore we are saved by love.

Reinhold Niebuhr

12

The Rewards of Love

John Dryden wrote, "Love is love's reward." And Kierkegaard observed, "To cheat oneself out of love ... is an eternal loss for which there is no reparation, either in time or eternity."

We conclude with a few thoughts on life's eternal reward: love.

The story of a love is not important — what is important is that one is capable of love. It is perhaps the only glimpse we are permitted of eternity.

Helen Hayes

Till it has loved, no man or woman can become itself.

Emily Dickinson

Love cures people — both the ones
who give it and the ones who receive it.

Karl Menninger

The love we give away is the only love
we keep.

Elbert Hubbard

Love is a mutual self-giving which ends
in self-recovery.

Bishop Fulton J. Sheen

To be capable of giving and receiving mature
love is as sound a criterion as we have
for the fulfilled personality.

Rollo May

Perfect love casteth out fear.

I John 4:18

Until I truly loved, I was alone.

Caroline Norton

One word frees us of all the weight
and pain of life: That word is love.

Sophocles

Take away love and our earth is a tomb.

Robert Browning

Love is Nature's second sun.

George Chapman

Real love is a permanently
self-enlarging experience.

M. Scott Peck

Love stretches your heart and makes you big inside.

Margaret Walker

To cheat oneself out of love is the most terrible deception.

Kierkegaard

A wise lover values not so much the gift
of the lover as the love of the giver.

Thomas à Kempis

It is astonishing how little one feels poverty
when one loves.

John Bulver

Who, being loved, is poor?

Oscar Wilde

He who is filled with love is filled
with God Himself.

St. Augustine

Passion makes all things alive
and significant.

Ralph Waldo Emerson

Intimacy is not simple. It's a great challenge
to our maturity. It's our greatest hope.

Leo Buscaglia

There is only one terminal dignity — love.

Helen Hayes

If your love be pure, simple, and well ordered,
you shall be free from bondage.

Thomas à Kempis

What is lovely never dies but passes
into other loveliness.

Thomas Bailey Aldrich

Old and true love never rusts.

Hebrew Proverb

He that loveth not
knoweth not God;
for God is love.

I John 4:8

A man is only as good as what he loves.

Saul Bellow

Better to have loved and lost
    than not to have loved at all.

Seneca

One makes mistakes: That is life.
But it is never quite a mistake to have loved.

Romain Rolland

One loves because he wills it, because it
gives him joy, because he knows that growth
and discovery of oneself depend upon it.

Leo Buscaglia

As selfishness and complaint pervert and
cloud the mind, so love with its joys clears
and sharpens the vision.

Helen Keller

The deepest truth blooms only
    from the deepest love.

Heinrich Heine

The greatest happiness of life
    is the conviction that we are loved —
        loved for ourselves, or rather,
            loved in spite of ourselves.

Victor Hugo

The best way to know God
    is to love many things.

Vincent van Gogh

When you come right down to it,
    the secret of having it all is loving it all.

Dr. Joyce Brothers

Let love be purified, and all the rest
    will follow. A pure love is thus, indeed,
    the panacea for all the ills of the world.

Henry David Thoreau

There is a land of the living and a land of the
dead and the bridge is love, the only survival,
    the only meaning.

Thornton Wilder

By the accident of fortune, a man may rule
    the world for a time, but by virtue of love
    he may rule the world forever.

Lao-tzu

Those who love deeply
never grow old; they may
die of old age, but they
die young.

Sir Arthur Wing Pinero

When love and skill work together, expect a masterpiece.

John Ruskin

Sources

Sources

George Ade 78
Aesop 86
Louisa May Alcott 19
Thomas Bailey Aldrich 145
Angelus Silesius 63
Henri Frédéric Amiel
    41, 66, 79, 96, 126
Margaret Anderson 72
Jean Anouilh 38
Aristotle 107, 128
W. H. Auden 112
St. Augustine 18, 57, 60, 143
Decimus Maximus Ausonius
    57
Jane Austen 76
Francis Bacon 110
James Baldwin 51
Lucille Ball 32
Aaron Beck 59, 70, 72, 96,
    121, 129, 131
Saul Bellow 147
Arnold Bennett 84
Erma Bombeck 76
Dietrich Bonhoeffer 122
Richard Brooks 78
Dr. Joyce Brothers 60, 149
Helen Gurley Brown 27
Elizabeth Barrett Browning
    50
Robert Browning 69, 140
Martin Buber 49
Pearl Buck 60
John Bulver 143
Leo Buscaglia 17, 26, 31, 34,
    39, 42, 47, 58, 60, 63, 72,
    95, 100, 117, 120, 144,
    148
Lord Byron 81
Sid Caesar 33
Eddie Cantor 56
Thomas Carlyle 23

Amy Carmichael 86
Dale Carnegie 85
Miguel de Cervantes 63
Coco Chanel 51, 70
George Chapman 140
Pierre Charron 86
G. K. Chesterton 50
Charles Churchill 85
Confucius 103, 118, 119
Norman Cousins 84, 99
The Dalai Lama 126
Tyne Daly 47
Bette Davis 65
Charles Dickens 95
Emily Dickinson 137
Benjamin Disraeli 22
Marjory Stoneman Douglas 29
Rudolf Dreikurs 129
John Dryden 135
Ralph Waldo Emerson 24, 34,
    44, 56, 69, 80, 105, 108,
    126, 144
Euripides 67
B. C. Forbes 115
Harry Emerson Fosdick
    98, 122
Viktor Frankl 26, 27, 119
Erich Fromm 24, 28, 37, 39,
    41, 43, 48, 56, 59, 116, 121
Thomas Fuller 69, 70
Eva Gabor 21, 34
Mohandas Gandhi 17, 18,
    52, 102
Kahlil Gibran 20, 23, 120
André Gide 124, 130
Louis Ginzberg 20
Goethe 58, 61, 73
Vincent van Gogh 52, 149
Thaddeus Golas 64
Sam Goldwyn 93
Baltasar Gracián 110, 118, 129

Sources

Robert Schuller 26
Seneca 80, 148
William Shakespeare 42, 45,
    109
Bishop Fulton J. Sheen 108,
    138
Percy Bysshe Shelley 83
Charles Simmons 71
Alexander Smith 27
Sophocles 139
Dr. Robert Sternberg 74
Robert Louis Stevenson
    22, 112
Henry Stimson 126
Mother Teresa 88, 121
William Makepeace
    Thackeray 86
Henry David Thoreau
    63, 66, 132, 150
James Thurber 131
Paul Tillich 34, 87, 90, 133
Leo Tolstoy 24
Paul Tournier 80, 82
Horace Traubel 69
Mark Twain 57, 77
Frank Tyger 90
Peter Ustinov 102
Henry Van Dyke 82
Vauvenargues 53
Voltaire 101
Margaret Walker 141
Justice Wallington 115
William Arthur Ward 109
Raquel Welch 91
Mae West 76
Betty White 94
John Greenleaf Whittier 121
Ella Wheeler Wilcox 132
Oscar Wilde 143
Thornton Wilder 150

David Wilkerson 47
William Wirt 78
William Wordsworth 83
Xenophon 92
Loretta Young 73, 85

About Wisdom Books

Wisdom Books chronicle memorable quotations in an easy-to-read style. Written by Criswell Freeman, this series provides inspiring, thoughtful and humorous messages from entertainers, athletes, scientists, politicians, clerics, writers and renegades. Each title focuses on a particular region or area of special interest.

Combining his passion for quotations with extensive training in psychology, Dr. Freeman revisits timeless themes such as perseverance, courage, love, forgiveness and faith.

"Quotations help us remember the simple yet profound truths that give life perspective and meaning," notes Freeman. "When it comes to life's most important lessons, we can all use gentle reminders."

About the Author

Criswell Freeman is a Doctor of Clinical Psychology living in Nashville, Tennessee. He is the author of *When Life Throws You a Curveball, Hit It* and *The Wisdom Series* from WALNUT GROVE PRESS.

The Wisdom Series
by Dr. Criswell Freeman

Regional Titles

Wisdom Made in America	ISBN 1-887655-07-7
The Book of Southern Wisdom	ISBN 0-9640955-3-X
The Wisdom of the Midwest	ISBN 1-887655-17-4
The Wisdom of the West	ISBN 1-887655-31-X
The Book of Texas Wisdom	ISBN 0-9640955-8-0
The Book of Florida Wisdom	ISBN 0-9640955-9-9
The Book of California Wisdom	ISBN 1-887655-14-X
The Book of New York Wisdom	ISBN 1-887655-16-6
The Book of New England Wisdom	ISBN 1-887655-15-8

Sports Titles

The Golfer's Book of Wisdom	ISBN 0-9640955-6-4
The Putter Principle	ISBN 1-887655-39-5
The Golfer's Guide to Life	ISBN 1-887655-38-7
The Wisdom of Southern Football	ISBN 0-9640955-7-2
The Book of Stock Car Wisdom	ISBN 1-887655-12-3
The Wisdom of Old-Time Baseball	ISBN 1-887655-08-5
The Book of Football Wisdom	ISBN 1-887655-18-2
The Book of Basketball Wisdom	ISBN 1-887655-32-8
The Fisherman's Guide to Life	ISBN 1-887655-30-1
The Tennis Lover's Guide to Life	ISBN 1-887655-36-0

Special Interest Titles

The Book of Country Music Wisdom	ISBN 0-9640955-1-3
Old-Time Country Wisdom	ISBN 1-887655-26-3
The Wisdom of Old-Time Television	ISBN 1-887655-64-6
The Cowboy's Guide to Life	ISBN 1-887655-41-7
The Wisdom of the Heart	ISBN 1-887655-34-4
The Guide to Better Birthdays	ISBN 1-887655-35-2
The Gardener's Guide to Life	ISBN 1-887655-40-9
Minutes from the Great Women's Coffee Club (by Angela Beasley)	ISBN 1-887655-33-6